a finger in derek jarman's mouth

simon maddrell

polari   poetry

time can worry others

digging, digging with my ink

sweat greening on a dry page

iron sculptures in a sketchbook

already filled, filled with music

seeping, seeping from its spine

derek jarman (1942–1994)

contents

a finger in derek jarman's mouth

where the shadow scatters, streaks on silver
clouds billow yards of fine cotton
wind howls through the dwindling mountains
drawn through the billboard promised land
these fooly wastes teasing mortality
the last gaseous bead in warm flat beer
glimpsing an exile passing geometric laughter
someone has painted the oak yellow

tied a ribbon with blood
fiery cherubs stalk the violet sky
where the lights talk and offer consolation
to death coming through mirrors
how you loved the worn shine, its wild hope
a postcard wishing you were [where you cannot be]

from Derek Jarman's *a finger in the fishes mouth*

dungeness

the driest body in england

an isolation

sagging shells

radiation in the bones

bleached and skeletal

leaves rotted

sickness blows through me

but the inside

full of

oozing

dog roses

sea kale

dried out

like tumbleweed

fucking like fairlight donkeys

sex kittens still scamper in

gorse passion

my body

where it remains

a threaded necklace

hanging

more of a joy than bother

my garden

red poppies splash

the landscape

rusting chains

water to gravel

dust to wind

after the bluebells turned to concrete

we turned left into yellow windows
his taste downed the chintz curtains
in dungeness — *the dangerous nose*

could smell its potential
gallons of bitumen paint
evaporating in a whiff just
as he wished one day for all

his works, the cottage will rot
plants shrivel gravel-blind
films self-combust like gorse
his signature on the grave slate

will wash, long after this decay
in concrete & radiation
he will remain
in the blue

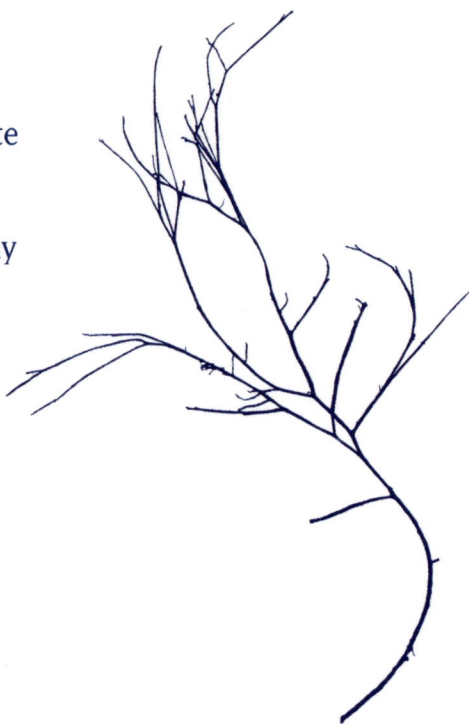

after Tilda Swinton

crambe maritima

anointed with a necklace of holey
stones and flint from the lowest
tide, a new life for driftwood in
a sea kale spring bloom, till now

a purple bud on a corky stem
protruding pink-edged pebbles
if only this were a metaphor for sex
dying away completely in winter

with a sticky honey scent
grief roots twenty feet deep
losing green fingers one-by-one
counting the weeks after new year
till splayed leaf hands turn to bone

paradise

faggots in my arms
gathered from the beach
instead of Heaven

my paradise — a garden
in ancient persian too —
though haunted by slugs

like the black cat brings
a mouse on his top lip
after its treasure chase

shadows skip with sprigs
of lavender on a shingle
beach, instead of heaven

phallus sculptura

hand-picked steel
blue-beaten brown

wood-drifted smooth
gaping holes flood

iron-twisted will
nailed to a cross

flotsam-jetsam
at the cottage

who is chosen
& who is not

first love

airman johnny takes me on a bike

I hold him in his pockets

and a bomb-damaged house

clinging to his pink & white

like on the road back home

valerian on the verge

which doesn't last long —

but there will be a second

flowering

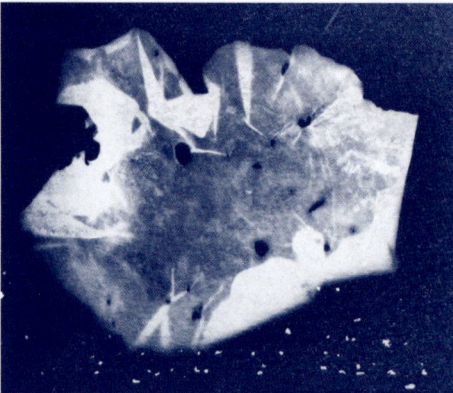

winter flowering

poor violet
violated for a rhyme

my heartsease
johnny-jump-up
a peach outlives

his hand

holds its stem
seeds-spunk-up
his abs

poor johnny
wanking for a dime

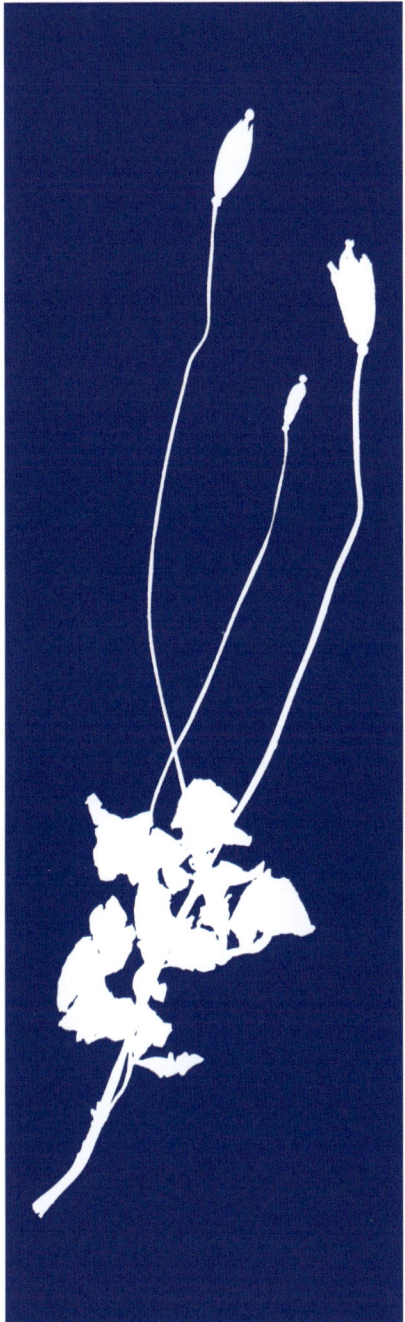

Honey Bees

i've never been stung from the hive
— except, by accident, the once,
which now i live with openly but
slowly dying down from its sting —
a coffin of railway sleepers

will serve me with honey —
my Hinney Beast of true love,
my Hydrogen Bomb of disease,
all still here after winter sleeps —
my dungeness gold, even when

i've lost the strength to lift
my combs, but not to stare at
my plants, feel sweetness on
my lips.

i.m. Keith Collins (aka HB/Hinney Beast)

almost the moon on a stick

a thin black sliver
life ticks through

the salted rust
worn out holes

bones of kale
where purple pops

the rabbits chew
like squirrel claws

floppy ears
beat bushy tails

the rats scuttle
with rings like trees

the snails slither death
with millions of teeth

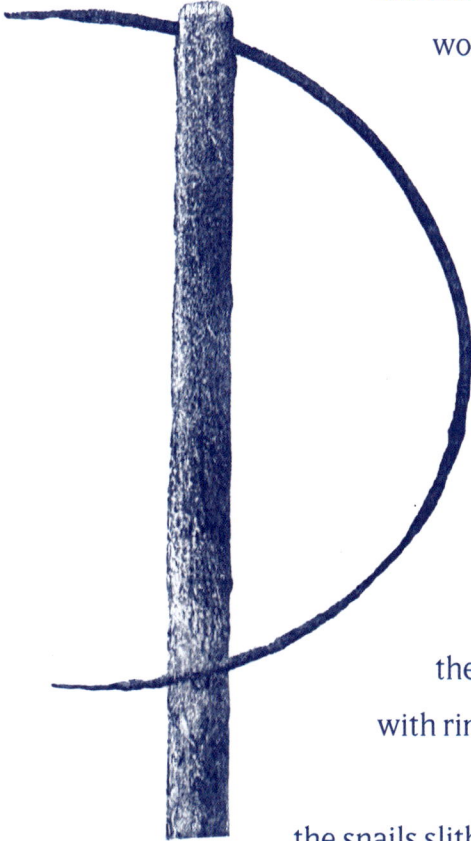

powered by HIV

like dungeness,

an overactive fuel

energy from atomic

cell destruction

a harsh wind laying

waste its beauty

a fission of dreams

drawings and plain

bloody-minded will

keep on trying

trying to keep on

smiling in slow motion

like those horsemen

riding the tide

BLUE BLUE BLUE BLUE BLUE BLUE BLUE BLUE BLUE BLUE
BLUE BLUE BLUE BLUE BLUE BLUE BLUE BLUE BLUE BLUE
BLUE BLUE BLUE BLUE BLUE BLUE BLUE COME IN   BLUE
BLUE BLUE BLUE BLUE BLUE BLUE BLUE BLUE BLUE BLUE
BLUE BLUE BLUE BLUE BLUE ASCEND   BLUE BLUE BLUE
BLUE BLUE BLUE BLUE BLUE BLUE BLUE BLUE BLUE BLUE
BLUE H.B. BLUE BLUE ARISE BLUE BLUE SIZE BLUE BLUE
BLUE BLUE BLUE BLUE BLUE BLUE BLUE QUEEN   BLUE
BLUE COME FORTH   BLUE BLUE BLUE BLUE BLUE BLUE
BLUE BLUE BLUE BLUE BLUE BLUE BLUE FUNK BLUE BLUE
BLUE BLUE MUFF BLUE BLUE BLUE BLUE BLUE BLUE BLUE
BLUE DIVE BLUE BLUE BLUE BLUE BLUE PSYCHOFAG BLUE
BLUE BLUE BLUE BLUE LOOK BLUE BLUE BLUE BLUE BLUE
BLUE BLUE BLUE BLUE BLUE BLUE BLUE BLUE BLUE BLUE
BLUE BLUE LOOK BLUE BLUE BLUE LOOK BLUE BLUE BLUE
BLUE BLUE BLUE BLUE BLUE BLUE BLUE BLUE BLUE BLUE
BLUE BLUE BLUE BLUE LOOK BLUE BLUE BLUE BLUE BLUE
BLUE BLUE BLUE BLUE BLUE BLUE BLUE BLUE BLUE BLUE
BLUE BLUE BLUE BLUE LOVE BLUE BLUE FADES   BLUE
BLUE BLUE BLUE BLUE BLUE BLUE BLUE BLUE BLUE BLUE
BLUE BUZZING   BLUE BLUE BLUE BLUE BLUE BLUE BLUE
BLUE BLUE BLUE BLUE HAZE BLUE BLUE SING BLUE BLUE
BLUE BLUE BLUE BLUE BLUE BLUE BLUE BLUE BLUE BLUE
BLUE BLUE HEART   BLUE BLUE BLUE BLUE BLUE BLUE
BLUE BLUE BLUE BLUE BLUE BLUE DREAMS   BLUE BLUE
BLUE COCK BLUE SUCKING   BLUE BLUE BLUE BLUE BLUE
BLUE BLUE CROWBLUE BLUE BLUE VOICES   BLUE BLUE
BLUE CAW BLUE BLUE BLUE BLUE BLUE BLUE BLUE BLUE
BLUE BLUE DAWNBLUE BLUE BLUE BLUE DEAD BLUE BLUE
BLUE BLUE BLUE BLUE BLUE BLUE BLUE BLUE BLUE BLUE

BLUE BLUE BLUE BLUE BLUE BLUE BLUE BLUE BLUE BLUE
BLUE BLUE OPEN DOOR BLUE BLUE BLUE BLUE BLUE BLUE
BLUE BLUE BLUE BLUE BLUE BLUE STONE BLUE BLUE
BLUE BLUE BLUE BLUE ROOM BLUE BLUE BLUE BLUE BLUE
BLUE BLUE BLUE BLUE BLUE BLUE AZURE BLUE BLUE
BLUE BLUE DIX BLUE BLUE BLUE BLUE BLUE DAWN
BLUE BLUE BLUE BLUE BLUE GROUND BLUE BLUE BLUE
BLUE BLUE BLUE BLUE GUN BLUE BLUE BLUE PANSY
BLUE BLUE BLUE BLUE BLUE BLUE BLUE BLUE BLUE BLUE
BLISS BLUE BLUE BLUE POWDER BLUE BLUE PILL BLUE
BLUE BLUE BLUE BLUE BLUE BLUE BLUE BLUE BLUE BLUE
BLUE BLUE BLUE BLUE BLUE BLUE ELECTRIC BLUE BLUE
BLUE BLUE BUTTERFLY BLUE BLUE BLUE BLUE BLUE BLUE
BLUE BLUE BLUE BLUE BORROWED BLUE BLUE BLUE
BLUE BLUE BLUE BLUE BLUE BLUE BLUE BLUE LIGHTBLUE
BLUE BLUE BLUE BEARDED BLUE BLUE BLUE BLUE BLUE
BLUE BLUE BLUE BLUE BLUE BLUE PERIWINKLE BLUE BLUE
BLUE BLUE CERULEAN BLUE BLUE BLUE BLUE BLUE BLUE
BLUE BLUE BLUE BLUE BLUE BLUE BLUE DUCK BLUE BLUE
BLUE BLUE BLUE GRAY BLUE BLUE BLUE BLUE BLUE BLUE
BLUE BLUE BLUE BLUE BLUE BLUE BLUE EYED BOY BLUE
BLUE BLUE BLUE BLUE BLUE BLUE PALE BLUE BLUE BLUE
BLUE BLUE DENIM BLUE BLUE BLUE BLUE BLUE BLUE
BLUE BLUE BLUE BLUE BLUE BLUE BLUE BLUE HEAT BLUE
ROBINEGG BLUE BLUE BLUE AURA BLUE BLUE BLUE BLUE
BLUE BLUE BLUE BLUE BLUE BLUE BLUE BLUE GREY BLUE
BLUE BLUE BLUE SUGAR BAG BLUE BLUE BLUE BLUE BLUE
BLUE BLUE BLUE BLUE BLUE SLATE BLUE BLUE BLUE BLUE
BLUE BLOOD BLUE BLUE BLUE BLUE BLUE BLUE BLUE
BLUE BLUE BLUE BLUE DARKNESS BLUE BLUE BLUE BLUE

BLUE BLUE BLUE BLUE BLUE BLUE BLUE BLUE BLUE BLUE
BLUE BLUE BLUE PILL BLUE BLUE BLUE BLUE BLUE BLUE
BLUE BLUE BLUE BLUE BLUEBELL BLUE BLUE BLUE BLUE
BLUE URANIAN BLUE BLUE BLUE CORNFLOWER BLUE
BLUE BLUE BLUE BLUE BLUE BLUE BLUE BLUE BLUE BLUE
BLUE BLUE BLUE BLUE BLUE BLUE BLUE BLUE BLUEPANIC
BLUE BLUE BLUE BLUE BLUEBOTTLE BLUE BLUE BLUE
BLUE BLUE BLUETS BLUE BLUE BLUE BLUE BLUE BLUE
BLUE BLUE BLUE BLUE BLUE BLUE BLUE BLUE BLUE BLUE
BLIZZARD BLUE BLUE BLUE BLUE BLUE BLUE BLUE BLUE
BLUE BLUE BLUE BLUE BLUE BLUE BLUE BLUE BLUE BLUE
BLUE BLUE VIOLET BLUE BLUE BLUE BLUE BLUE BLUE
BLUE BLUE BLUE BLUE BLUE BUGLOSS BLUE BLUE BLUE
BLUE BLUE BLUE BLUE BLUE BLUE BLUE BLUE BLUE BLUE
BLUE BLUE BLUE BLUE DELPHINIUM BLUE BLUE BLUE BLUE
BLUE ROYALBLUE BLUE BLUE BLUE BLUE BLUE BLUE BLUE
BLUE AIR FORCE BLUE BLUE BLUE BLUE BLUE BLUE BLUE
BLUE BLUE BLUE BLUE SAGE BLUE BLUE BLUE BLUE BLUE
BLUE BLUE BLIND BLUE BLUE BLUE BLUE DEEP BLUE BLUE
BLUE BLUE BLUE BLUE BLUE BLUE BLUE BLUE BLUE BLUE
BLUE WINTER BLUE BLUE BLUE LIBERTY BLUE BLUE
BLUE HYACINTH BLUE BLUE BLUE BLUE BLUE BLUE BLUE
BLUE BLUE BLUE BLUE BLUE BLUE UNIVERSAL BLUE BLUE
BLUE YVES BLUE BLUE BLUE BLUE BLUE BLUE BLUE BLUE
BLUE KLEIN BLUE BITTER SLOE BLUE LOVE BLUE BLUE
BLUE BLUE BLUE BLUE BLUE BLUE BLUE BLUE BLUE BLUE
BLUE VOID BLUE BLUE BLUE ETERNITY BLUE BLUE BLUE
VOID VOID VOID BLUE BLUE BLUE BLUE BLUE BLUE BLUE
BLUE VOID BLUE BLUE BLUE BLUE BLUE BLUE WILD BLUE
BLUE BLUE BLUE BLUE BLUE BLUE BLUE BLUE YONDER

BLUE BLUE BLUE BLUE BLUE BLUE BLUE BLUE BLUE BLUE
BLUE BELLADONNA   BLUE BLUE BLUE BLUE BLUE BLUE
BLUE BLUE BLUE BLUE BLUE BLUE BLIND   BLUE BLUE
BLUE BLUE BLUE BLUE HIGH BLUE BLUE BLUE BLUE BLUE
BLOTS BLUE BLUE BLUE BLUE BLUE BLUE BLUE BLUE
BLUE BLUE BLUE LOW BLUE BLUE LINES   BLUE BLUE
BLUE UNIVERSAL BLUE LOST BLUE BLUE BLUE BLUE BLUE
BLUE BLUE BLUE BLUE BOYS BLUE BLUE BLUE BLUE BLUE
BLUE BLUE BLUE BLUE BLUE BLUE SALT BLUE BLUE BLUE
FLASHES   BLUE BLUE LINES BLUE BLUE LIPS   BLUE BLUE
BLUE BLUE BLUE BLUE DEAD BLUE BLUE BLUE BLUE BLUE
BLUE BLUE BLUE BLUE BLUE GOOD BLUE BLUE BLUE BLUE
BLUE BLUE BLUE BLUE BLUE BLUE LOOKING   BLUE BLUE
KISS   BLUE BLUE BLUE BLUE BLUE BLUE BLUE BLUE BLUE
BLUE LIPS   BLUE BLUE BLUE BLUE BLUE COOL BLUE BLUE
BLUE BLUE EYES BLUE BLUE BLUE BLUE BLUE BLUE BLUE
RASHES   BLUE BLUE SOCKS   BLUE BLUE BLUE BLUE
BLUE BLUE HIVES   BLUE BLUE BLUE BLUE BLUE BLUE
BLUE BLUE BLUE BLUE BLUE BLUE DRUGS   BLUE BLUE
BAD   BLUE BLUE BLUE MIST BLUE BLUE BLUE BLUE BLUE
BLUE BLUE BLUE BLUE BLUE BLUE BLUE PAIN BLUE BLUE
BLUE BLOOD   BLUE BLUE RAYS BLUE MADE BLUE BLUE
BLUE BLUE BLUE BLUE BLUE BLUE BLUE TANGIBLE   BLUE
BLUE BANKS   BLUE BLUE SPARKS   BLUE BLUE BLUE
BLUE BLUE DEEP BLUE BLUE BLUE BLUE BLUE BLUE BLUE
BLUE BLUE BLUE BLUE BLUE BLUE UPON BLUE BLUE BLUE
BLUE BLUE BLUE IN TIME   BLUE BLUE BLUE BLUE BLUE
BLUE BLUE BLUE BLUE BLUE BLUE BLUE YOUR BLUE BLUE
BLUE BLUE FORGOTTEN BLUE BLUE BLUE BLUE BLUE BLUE
BLUE BLUE BLUE BLUE BLUE BLUE BLUE BLUE   GRAVE

the visitors

a host of lichens comes
stubble on a rock-hard chest

mosses too, a muted softness
licks, caresses the feet

like in bed after sex
even the rarest of beings

i see them in the wind
i hear fungus in my mouth

life confirmed as	**a time bomb**
a poisoned chalice	in a ghetto
a chastity ring	frightened &
three-lettered	unhappy people
long-sleeved	who can't tell the truth
sick-ugly	to others & ourselves
throbbing	my whole body
so well-cloaked	a struggle
if only I knew	how to make life
a chosen silence	open & acceptable
sequinned boots	to disclose my secret
awful socks	& survive Margaret Thatcher

HIV   STIGMA

	MEANS
I HAVE	
	BECOME
A LETHAL	
	SECRET
WEAPON	
I DETEST	
	PRIVACY
TERMINAL ILLNESS	
	ELABORATELY
STOPS	
	MURDERS
TIME	
	ITSELF

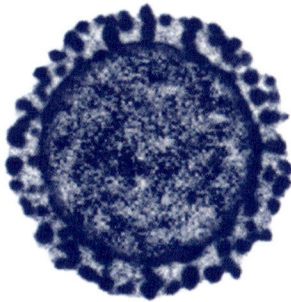

the last of birthdays

a thistle-looking man,
four limbs in spiny stems
a sainthood enthroned, dry
skin prickling, dense flowers

like closed eyes, blind too.
the rest of the inevitable
was hiding under his cottage
table shrouded in cloth.

quietus encroached
his melting mind
the wastes of his body
thorny edges in his soul

re-emerged from the grave
his coffin-seeding thistle
grew pink & purple buds
too late for liver & blood

but still making art
like hampstead heath
bending rules of what
can be done & where.

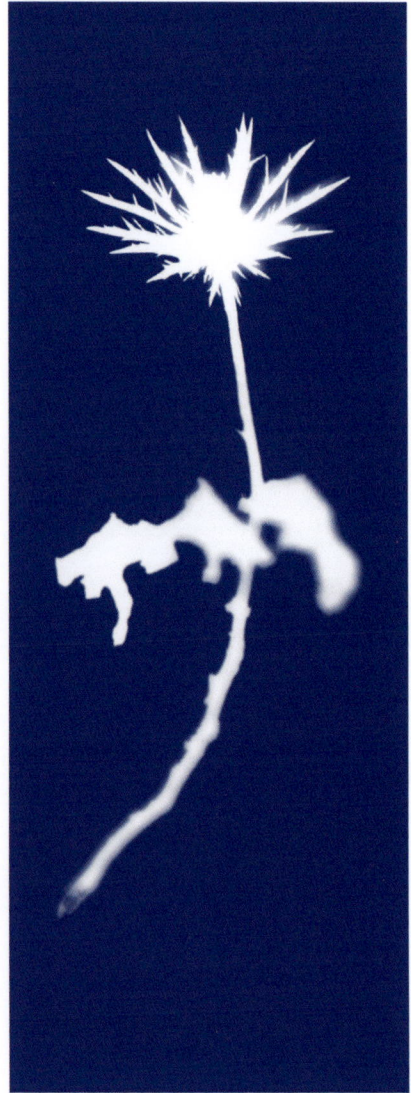

after Alexandra Symons Sutcliffe

Derek Jarman died of AZT

i mean it, but do not sue me
you cannot prove it is not true
he was not the only one
to die, after a treatment that aids
& abets its own outcome
the (non-)charitable claim
you did the best you could

to find what you needed
to say about its remedial features
for consultants to prescribe
in fourfold doses & earlier too
but you will not sue me
we know exactly what you fixed
you did the best you could

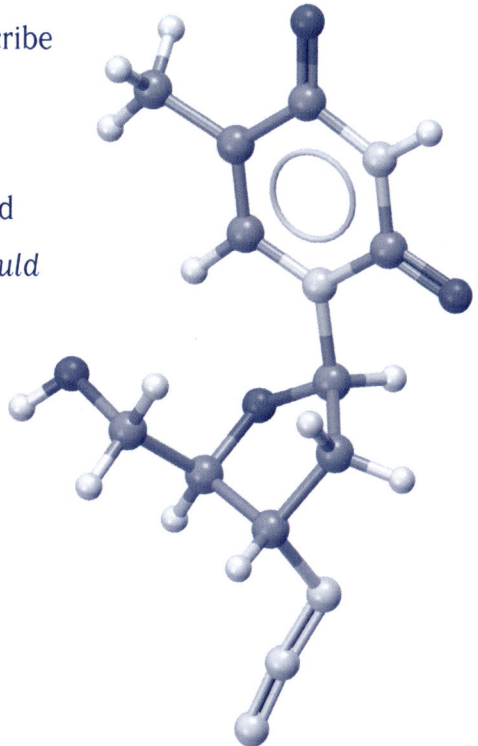

famous for fairlight donkeys

for fame has its own walls & fences & dances
a famously brazen film director robbed by time
of today's cinematic freedoms. a garden infused
throughout chelsea shows off the world's largest
shingle beach. *oryctolagus cuniculus*, a devil in
disguise, neither whistled nor named, a talismanic
doom for fishermen & their sea kale plots of land.
The home to a third of britain's plants amidst
standing stones & dragon's teeth, where duck-
billed dinosaurs grazed & browsed. these shores
of herbivores i'd never heard of — except for
those clapboard cottages & clapboard films.
the only imprint from him — for some, maybe
will be — a stack of pebbles bought from B&Q.

for Neil Bartlett

never going to heaven

time eludes us	as it bothers others
instead	deceives loneliness
shadow's shadow	glows with life
sodium & ruby light	like dungeness
on a humming night	popping shots
a rattling rattle	in dark doorways
like dungeness	two-by-two
sunshine frames	through the cottage
stinking hawksbeard	floating on passion
lying dead still	asking if we cruise
in a beige suit	or shy away
like a jay	in a blue flash

War Requiem

he kneels before limpness
kisses their spread-eagled
body on the bed
of barbed wire but nothing
except for the blood drips
pricked by a harsher steel
love's belly a dead smile.

he stands broken & pale
the other-side soldier
limp & departed from
his vengeful bayonet
sunk in red flurries
a grasped cornet lies
its choked music smells

the thick green odour of last
week's man, their breath still
murmurs in that black snow
imprinted in chalk trenches
worrying the torn sky
like pity distilled
in his patient mind.

after Wilfred Owen, Benjamin Britten and Derek Jarman

concerted effort

britannia paraded on the stage
dressed in drag with soldiers in
ill-fitting dresses and trench-less
boots. a drummer boy appears
in a woollen jumper and a skull
cap — his round mouth crimson
with an unknowing look.

out of battle it seemed he had
escaped those goodbye faces
— his own camouflage-
painted but with blusher
showing us his hiding
lipstick smudged memories
shadow on the eyes.

after Wilfred Owen and Derek Jarman

the cruel & unnecessary

perversion of innocence, as if
The Garden was the genesis
of original sin — the trotted
tropes of adam & steve.

The Last of England's claim to
decency — the naked shame of
denying queer rights to kiss & piss
or pretending a family is blood.

gethsemane, a requiem
for fateful war, prayers too late
to mop bleeding bones, to stop
the hangman in his chest, crying
the nectar of a rose.

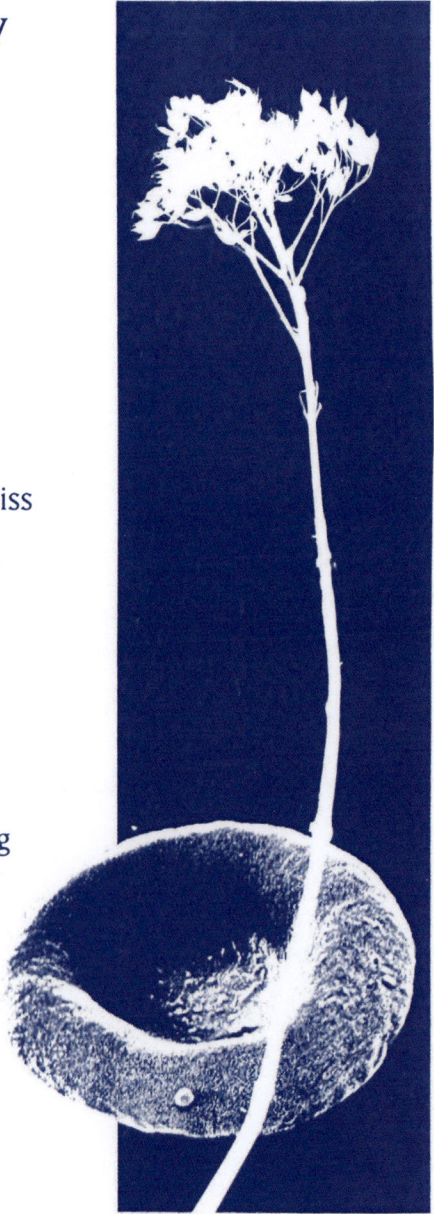

there are no walls or fences

in this landscape where
the toughest fishermen turn into
desolate shingle   stony squabbles
round   the   sage-green   sea   kale
and yellow sedum.   red poppy
is   broken   only   by   this   wind
taking   hold   and   the   constant
bringing in of the afternoon catch.

my   garden's   horizons   are   gulls
the   wind   here   paving   the   way
for   more   silence   than   anywhere
in britain sunlight is desert grasses
its   boundaries   the   blue   bugloss.

a found poem from derek jarman

dear derek jarman

i too have hiv
but much too late for death
— not too early to be saved.
i've built a garden somewhere
but you did it nowhere. you said

my garden's boundaries are the horizon
but you didn't only mean
dungeness. when you said
there are no walls or fences,
you weren't describing

our inward journey
or casting a shadow across
the floor of Heaven. after you
made those films, you don't know
rivulets ran through my parched

grass. as if being banned and
disliked is a pinnacle
after all. you refused to die
without the sun rising
without stones threaded

and hung in a garden
that grew out of nothing
without going quietly
smiling in slow motion
an iceberg dropping

from the sky.
the ripples still
licking shingle
in a one-
way tide.

when i visit prospect cottage

i'll take you five dried yellow roses
(because one of them fell apart).
i'll repaint the wall on the side
with *The Sunne Rising*

and blame black tar for making me
cry, then forget what it was
i came here to escape.

twice or thrice i loved before
i knew your face & name, now
smelling wings somewhere
between air & angels.

after John Donne

notes

'time can worry others' is by the author, though *time can worry others* is a Jarman quote.

'a finger in derek jarman's mouth' — a found poem (except for "tied a ribbon with blood") from the poetry book, *a finger in the fishes mouth*, by Derek Jarman.

'after the bluebells turned to concrete' inspired by a story from Tilda Swinton (*Derek Jarman's Modern Nature*, John Hansard Gallery, 2021).

'winter flowering' — *Poor violet, violated for a rhyme* is from *Chroma* (Century, 1994).

'HBs' — 'Hinney [sic] Beast' and HB was Jarman's nickname for Keith Collins.

'[BLUE]' — Found words from the *Blue* film script and the book *Chroma*, plus names of plants in Prospect Cottage garden, and blue shades from various colour charts.

'powered by HIV' — *Smiling in Slow Motion* is the title of Jarman's posthumously published journals 1991—1994, taken from Jarman's scrapbook of the film *Sebastiane* where a photo of the titular character coming out of the sea has the same by-line.

'life confirmed as a time bomb' — the right-hand column is based on interviews with Jarman, including *Face to Face: Jeremy Isaacs talks to Derek Jarman*, 15 March 1993.

'HIV STIGMA' is a found poem from Derek Jarman's words, *ibid*.

'famous for fairlight donkeys' — a nickname for rabbits used by Keith Collins (thanks to Neil Bartlett, who also gifted me the comment about B&Q).

'the last of birthdays' inspired by a story by Alexandra Symons Sutcliffe (*Derek Jarman's Modern Nature*, John Hansard Gallery, 2021).

'there are no walls or fences' A found sonnet reordered from the diary entry of 1 January 1989 in *Modern Nature* (Century, 1991).

acknowledgements

'dear derek jarman' 'after the bluebells turned to concrete' 'paradise' 'HBs' 'powered by HIV' 'the cruel & unnecessary' 'the last of birthdays' 'when i visit prospect cottage' appeared in *Long Poem Magazine*, November 2023.

'life confirmed as a time bomb' appeared in *Poetry Wales*, Issue 58.1, Summer 2022.

'*crambe maritima*' 'first love' 'the visitors' appeared in *Ambit*, AMBIT 246, 2022.

'dungeness' appeared in *Elements: Natural & The Supernatural*, Fawn Press, Dec. 2021.

'there are no walls or fences' appeared in *Impossible Archetype Journal*, Issue 9, 2021.

cyanotypes

Artwork references (page number in brackets): (3) Red hornweed, *Ceramium virgatum*; (4) Carrageen, *Chondrus crispus*; (8) Slender wart weed, *Gracilaria gracilis*; (9) Sea kale, *Crambe maritima*; (12) Sea lettuce, *Ulva lactua*; (13) Welsh poppy, *Papaver cambricum*; (15) Sculpture from the garden at Prospect Cottage; (22) Globe thistle, *Echinops*; (23) HIV molecule; (24) Sea holly, *Eryngium alpinum*; (25) Ball-and-stick model of a zidovudine molecule, $C10H13N5O4$, also known as AZT; (30) Red blood cell and Stonecrop, *Hylotelephium*; (33) Prospect Cottage.

Thanks to Ian Montgomery at Positive East and Adam Rose at Wellcome Collection. Cyanotypes created with help from Matthew David @mattdavidartist

bibliography

A finger in the fishes mouth, Bettiscombe Press, 1972 and Test Centre, 2014.

Modern Nature, Century, 1991 / Vintage Classics, Penguin, 2018.

At Your Own Risk, Hutchinson, 1992 / Vintage Classics, Penguin, 2019.

Chroma, Century, 1994 / Vintage Classics, Penguin, 2019.

Derek Jarman, Blue: Das Buch zum Film, Verlag Martin Schmitz, 1994.

derek jarman's garden, Thames & Hudson Ltd, 1995.

Smiling in Slow Motion, Vintage, 2001 / Vintage Classics, Penguin, 2017.

Derek Jarman's Sketchbooks, Thames & Hudson Ltd, 2013.

Derek Jarman PROTEST! Irish Museum of Modern Art/Thames & Hudson Ltd, 2020.

Derek Jarman's Modern Nature, John Hansard Gallery, 2021.

'Simon Maddrell is a poet who knows Derek Jarman's work both intimately and deeply, and in this new collection he has taken words from Derek's diaries, images from the films and colours from that famously wild and stony Dungeness garden — and re-edited them into a loving, furious and gorgeously queer act of homage'
— **Neil Bartlett**, author of *Address Book* and *The Disappearance Boy*

'Brought back to us through weather and plant life, and in his works across multiple media, Derek Jarman becomes a celestial mirror ball, radiating inspiration from the heart of this poem-shrine lovingly "filled with music". Taking up the torch of Jarman's queer and HIV/AIDS art activism, Simon Maddrell declines the time-stamp of mortality and the diminutions of marginalisation, as his hero before him "refused to die/ without the sun rising". Also exploring his own poz status, Maddrell powerfully honours the generative nurture inherent to creative community, showing irrefutably how our lives are made more whole by art-making and receiving'
— **alice hiller**, author of *bird of winter*, shortlisted for the Forward Prize, 2021

'*a finger in derek jarman's mouth* is a tribute to Derek Jarman's home and garden at Prospect Cottage, plus a recognition of his pivotal role as an AIDS and queer activist/artist. Jarman courageously battled HIV, along with its stigma and shame. This homage stands as a testament to his enduring legacy. As someone close to Derek, it's heartening to see his impact remembered in such a moving manner'
— **Peter Tatchell**, human rights activist

'One of the most radical figures in queer culture honoured by the most propulsive of queer poets. Read this, and remember'
— **Joelle Taylor**, author of *C+nto and Othered Poems*, winner of the TS Eliot Prize for Poetry, 2021